The mighty Mississippi
Bauer, Marion Dan Quiz#: 114585
AR PTS: 0.5   RL: 2.7

Wonders of America

The Mighty Mississippi

For Brannon, of course!—M. D. B.

To Emma—J. G. W.

o🍵

ALADDIN PAPERBACKS
An imprint of Simon & Schuster Children's Publishing Division
1230 Avenue of the Americas, New York, NY 10020
Text copyright © 2007 by Marion Dane Bauer
Illustrations copyright © 2007 by John Wallace

Designed by Christopher Grassi
The text of this book was set in Century Old Style.
Manufactured in the United States of America
First Aladdin Paperbacks edition March 2007
2 4 6 8 10 9 7 5 3
Library of Congress Cataloging-in-Publication Data
Bauer, Marion Dane.
The mighty Mississippi / by Marion Dane Bauer ; illustrated by John
Wallace.—1st Aladdin Paperbacks ed.
p. cm.—(Ready-to-read) (Wonders of America)
ISBN-13: 978-0-689-86950-1 (pbk)
ISBN-10: 0-689-86950-9 (pbk)
ISBN-13: 978-0-689-86951-8 (library)
ISBN-10: 0-689-86951-7 (library)
1. Mississippi River—Juvenile literature. 2. Mississippi River—History—
Juvenile literature. 3. Mississippi River—Geography—Juvenile literature.
I. Wallace, John, 1966– ill. II. Title. III. Series.
F351.B38 2007
977—dc22
2006000960

The Mighty Mississippi

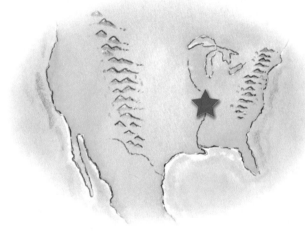

By **Marion Dane Bauer**

Illustrated by **John Wallace**

Ready-to-Read
ALADDIN
New York London Toronto Sydney

The Mississippi River
has many names.

The Mighty Mississippi.

Father of Waters.

Big Muddy.

Old Man River.

The name Mississippi
comes from an Indian word,
mesipi.
Mesipi means Big River.

The Big River begins
in northern Minnesota
near Lake Itasca.

It flows more than 2,300 miles
to the Gulf of Mexico.

11

It gathers water
from all the land west
to the Rocky Mountains.

It also gathers water
from all the land east
to the Appalachian Mountains.

Indians used light canoes
made of birch bark
to travel the Mississippi.

The first whites used
dugout canoes.
These canoes were
dug out of a whole tree trunk.

They were heavy
and hard to steer.

To carry goods on the river
whites made flatboats
and keelboats.
The flatboats were
very heavy and very hard
to steer.

The keelboats were
only a little better.

Finally, in 1807,
Robert Fulton made
the first steamboat.

Soon after that
steamboats were used
on the Mississippi.

25

Today barges move
up and down the river.

They are not fast.
But they move much
grain or corn or coal
for little cost.

The Mississippi River
divides east from west.

It carries cargo
north and south.

It truly is a great river.

Interesting Facts about the Mississippi River

★ The first white man to see the Mississippi River came from Spain. His name was Alonzo Alvarez de Pineda. In 1519 he sailed into the mouth of the Mississippi.

★ The first white man to actually travel on the Mississippi River was Hernando de Soto, who crossed the river in 1541 near what is now Memphis, Tennessee.

★ The first white man to find what he thought was the source of the Mississippi was Henry Schoolcraft. In 1832 he followed the river to a lake that he named Lake Itasca. Actually, the Mississippi has no single source. It begins from many small streams in northern Minnesota.

★ The reason the Mississippi is so muddy is that it wanders. It has time to loosen and pick up topsoil. It drops 500 million tons of dirt into the sea every year. It drops much more along the river's banks.

★ One of our most famous American writers was a riverboat pilot on the Mississippi. His name was Samuel Clemens, but he used Mark Twain as a pen name. He chose *mark twain* because that was a call used on the steamboats. It meant the water was twelve feet deep. That was deep enough for the boat to pass safely.